PHILIPPE LEGENDRE

W9-AHU-579

# KIDS CAN DRAW

# Forest Animals

CORA J. BELDEN LIBRARY
33 Church Street
Rocky Hill, CT 06067
WITHDRAWN

Walter Foster Publishing, Inc.
23062 La Cadena Drive
Laguna Hills, CA 92653 USA
ISBN 1-56010-270-5

© 1997, Editions Fleurus, Paris.
Text on pages 4-24 © 1997, Walter Foster Publishing, Inc. All rights reserved.
Original title *J'apprends á dessiner les animaux de la forêt,* © 1992, Editions Fleurus, Paris.

## Attention Parents and Teachers

All children can draw a circle, a square, or a triangle…which means that they can also learn to draw a bear, squirrel, or hedgehog! The KIDS CAN DRAW learning method is easy and fun. Children will learn a technique and a vocabulary of shapes that will form the basis for all kinds of drawing.

Pictures are created by combining geometric shapes to form a mass of volumes and surfaces. From this stage, children can give character to their sketches with straight, curved, or broken lines.

With just a few strokes of the pencil, a forest animal will appear—and with the addition of color, the picture will be real work of art!

The KIDS CAN DRAW method offers a real apprenticeship in technique and a first look at composition, proportion, shapes, and lines. The simplicity of this method ensures that the pleasure of drawing is always the most important factor.

## About Philippe Legendre

French painter, engraver, and illustrator, Philippe Legendre also runs a school of art for children aged 6–14 years. Legendre frequently spends time in schools and has developed this method of learning so that all children can discover the artist within themselves.

# Helpful Tips

1. Each picture is made up of simple geometric shapes, which are illustrated at the top of the left-hand page. This is called the **Vocabulary of Shapes.** Encourage children to practice drawing each shape before starting their pictures.

2. Suggest children use a pencil to do their sketches. This way, if they don't like a particular shape, they can just erase it and try again.

3. A dotted line indicates that the line should be erased. Have children draw the whole shape and then erase the dotted part of the line.

4. Once children finish their drawings, they can color them with crayons, colored pencils, or felt-tip markers. They may want to go over the lines with a black pencil or pen.

## Now let's get started!

The round bear hunts for honey…

in hives up in the trees.

With his thick and shaggy coat,

he doesn't mind the bees.

# **B**ear

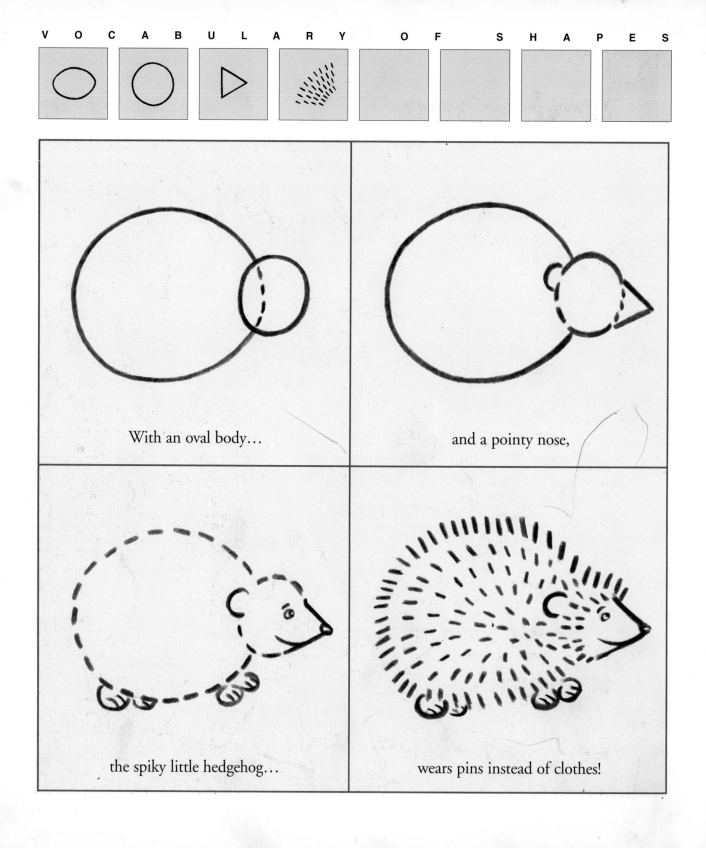

With an oval body…

and a pointy nose,

the spiky little hedgehog…

wears pins instead of clothes!

# Hedgehog

# Fox

The long-necked deer…

hides among the trees.

When there's a noise,

she quickly flees.

# Deer

Make three round balls…

and a tail with a curl.

Next thing you know,

you've made a squirrel!

# Squirrel

With triangle teeth…

and a mask of black,

the wolf is known…

to hunt in packs.

# Wolf

With circles on her coat and face,

the lynx looks like a cat...

from outer space!

# Lynx

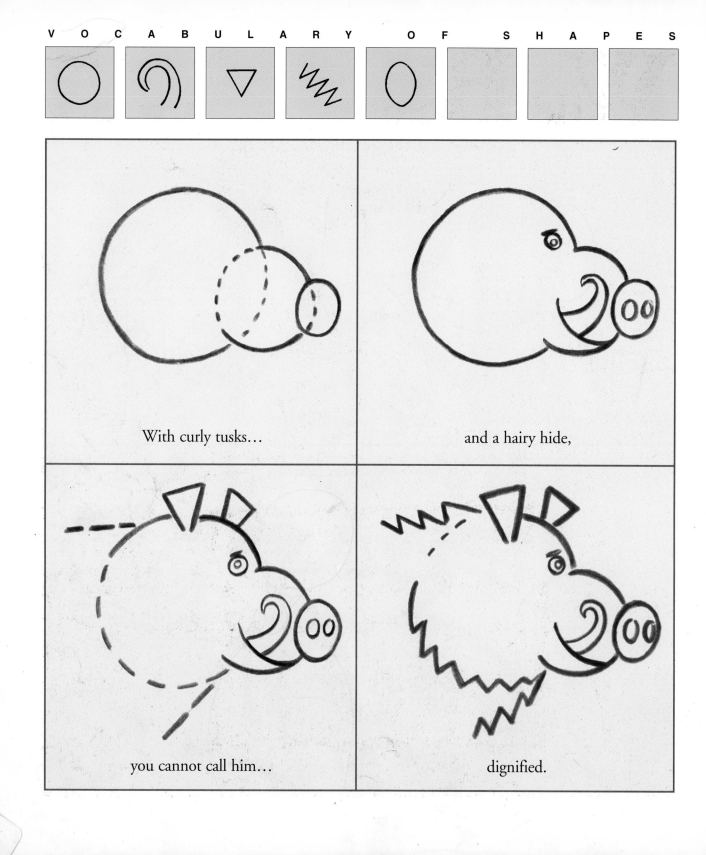

With curly tusks…

and a hairy hide,

you cannot call him…

dignified.

# **W**ild **B**oar

# VOCABULARY OF SHAPES

They say the owl…

is very wise…

with triangle feathers…

and circle eyes.

# O<sub>wl</sub>

In the forest you have drawn, the animals are on the prowl.

You can make the wise owl hoot and the fierce wolf growl.

# Draw-along fun for children!

With the **"I Can Draw"** series, kids ages 6 and up will have hours of fun drawing amazing pictures of all the things they like best—animals, cartoons, creepy creatures, race cars, and more. Each book is full of colorful step-by-step illustrations with easy-to-follow instructions, explaining how to draw almost anything from basic shapes kids already know, such as circles, squares, triangles, and ovals. Each 40-page book includes 8 pages of grid paper.

# More step-by-step fun for young artists!

Our 6 **"I Can Draw"** Drawing Kits come with an instruction book and all the materials kids need for drawing their favorite subjects. Each kit includes colored pencils, sharpener, eraser, and grid paper pad. These handy kits make great gifts for home, school, or travel.

*Walter Foster™*

For a free catalog, write to: Walter Foster Publishing, Inc. 23062 La Cadena Drive, Laguna Hills, CA 92653. Or call (800) 426-0099.